COUNTRY PROFILES

JAPAN

BY MARTY GITLIN

BLASTOFF!
DISCOVERY

BELLWETHER MEDIA • MINNEAPOLIS, MN

Blastoff! Discovery launches a new mission: reading to learn. Filled with facts and features, each book offers you an exciting new world to explore!

This edition first published in 2018 by Bellwether Media, Inc.

No part of this publication may be reproduced in whole or in part without written permission of the publisher.
For information regarding permission, write to Bellwether Media, Inc., Attention: Permissions Department,
5357 Penn Avenue South, Minneapolis, MN 55419.

Library of Congress Cataloging-in-Publication Data

Names: Gitlin, Marty, author.
Title: Japan / by Marty Gitlin.
Description: Minneapolis, MN : Bellwether Media, Inc., [2018]
| Series: Blastoff! Discovery: Country Profiles | Includes
bibliographical references and index. | Audience: Grades 3-8.
| Audience: Ages 7-13.
Identifiers: LCCN 2016057459 (print) | LCCN 2016057541
    (ebook) | ISBN 9781626176843 (hardcover : alk. paper)
    | ISBN 9781681034140 (ebook)
Subjects: LCSH: Japan–Juvenile literature.
Classification: LCC DS806 .G54 2018 (print) | LCC DS806
    (ebook) | DDC 952–dc23
LC record available at https://lccn.loc.gov/2016057459

Editor: Christina Leaf   Designer: Brittany McIntosh

Printed in the United States of America, North Mankato, MN.

TABLE OF CONTENTS

MOUNT FUJI
FUJIYOSHIDA

A plane begins its **descent** toward Shizuoka Airport. The passengers can see nothing but the clouds that blanket the sky. Suddenly, the snow-peaked **volcano** Mount Fuji appears, rising above the clouds. Towering 12,388 feet (3,776 meters) above the flat ground, *Fuji-san* is the highest mountain in Japan.

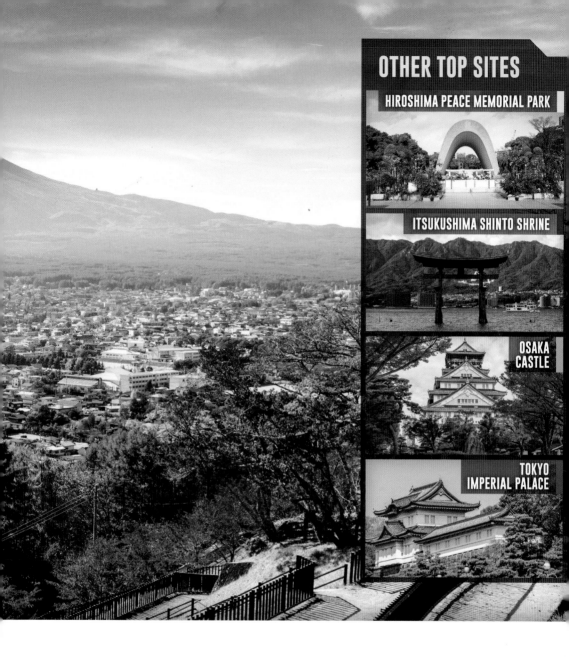

OTHER TOP SITES

HIROSHIMA PEACE MEMORIAL PARK

ITSUKUSHIMA SHINTO SHRINE

OSAKA CASTLE

TOKYO IMPERIAL PALACE

Several travelers are looking forward to climbing the **dormant** volcano, which has not erupted since 1707. They hope to witness a beautiful sunrise from the peak. Others will view it with awe as they speed by in a train. This is the majesty of Japan!

5

RUSSIA

HOKKAIDO

SAPPORO

NORTH
KOREA

SEA
OF JAPAN

HONSHU

SOUTH
KOREA

KYOTO

KOBE

JAPAN

TOKYO

MT. FUJI

SHIKOKU

KYUSHU

OSAKA

N
W E
S

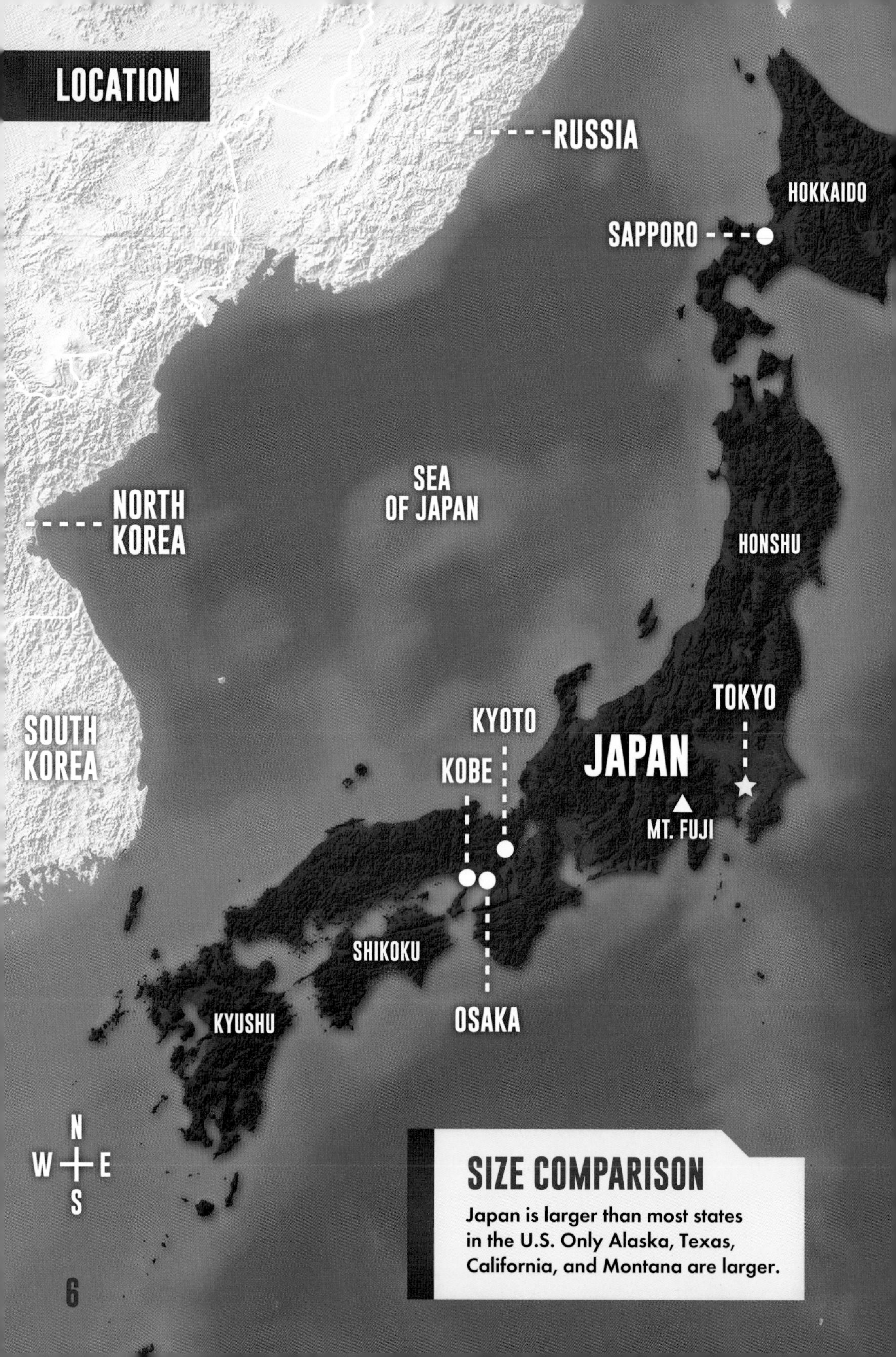

SIZE COMPARISON

Japan is larger than most states
in the U.S. Only Alaska, Texas,
California, and Montana are larger.

Japan is a long, narrow Asian nation consisting of 6,852 islands. The country covers 145,914 square miles (377,915 square kilometers). Tokyo, the capital, rests near the east coast. It is located on Honshu, the largest of four main islands that cover nearly all of Japan's land area. The others are Hokkaido, Shikoku, and Kyushu.

The country is surrounded by the Pacific Ocean to its east. Russia, North Korea, and South Korea sit across the Sea of Japan to the west. Japan owns the Ryukyu Islands to the south and the Bonin Islands to its southeast.

LANDSCAPE AND CLIMATE

Japan is a mountainous country. The mountains are covered by dense forests. The highest mountain range, the Japanese Alps, runs through central Honshu. Major cities are found in low areas such as the Kanto **Plain** in eastern Honshu. Many of Japan's islands have active volcanoes.

N
W+E
S

■ = JAPANESE ALPS ■ = KANTO PLAIN

JAPANESE ALPS
HAKUBA

KANTO PLAIN
GUNMA

SADO ISLAND
SEA OF JAPAN, NIIGATA

TOKYO
Average seasonal highs and lows

JANUARY
HIGH: 46 °F (8 °C)
LOW: 36 °F (2 °C)

APRIL
HIGH: 63 °F (17 °C)
LOW: 50 °F (10 °C)

JULY
HIGH: 82 °F (28 °C)
LOW: 72 °F (22 °C)

OCTOBER
HIGH: 68 °F (20 °C)
LOW: 59 °F (15 °C)

°F = degrees Fahrenheit
°C = degrees Celsius

Weather varies by region and season. Along the Sea of Japan, winters are rainy in the south and snowy in the north. The Pacific coast gets dry winds in the winter and heavy rain in the summer. The nation is often threatened with natural disasters, including volcanic eruptions and earthquakes. Giant **tsunamis** and stormy **typhoons** come from the ocean.

Over the years, construction and development have destroyed some wildlife **habitats** in Japan. But the country remains home to hundreds of animal species. Throughout most of Japan, snow monkeys sleep in trees and bathe in hot springs to get warm. Brown bears roam the mountains of Hokkaido. Endangered Japanese cranes nest in the protected Kushiro Marsh.

Sea turtles lay eggs on the beaches of southern islands. On the Amami Islands, rabbits scamper to avoid predators. **Venomous** pit vipers also slither through the islands' forests.

- - - BROWN BEAR

JAPANESE CRANE

JAPANESE PIT VIPER

SIKA DEER

SEEKING THE SIKA

Japan is home to more sika deer than any other country. The sika are known for their white spots in the summer.

SNOW MONKEYS
BATHING IN HOT SPRINGS

JAPANESE MACAQUE (SNOW MONKEY)

Life Span: 6 years; up to 32 years
Red List Status: least concern

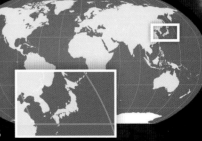

Japanese macaque range =

LEAST CONCERN	NEAR THREATENED	VULNERABLE	ENDANGERED	CRITICALLY ENDANGERED	EXTINCT IN THE WILD	EXTINCT
▲						

JAPANESE ADDITION

The Japanese add "san" to the end of names to show respect when talking to others. For example, a person with the last name Tanaka would be addressed as Tanaka-san.

Nearly 127 million people make Japan their home. Almost all are **native** to the country. A small number moved from South Korea, North Korea, and China.

Japanese is the language spoken by almost all of the population. Religion in the country is more **diverse**. Most Japanese people practice **Shintoism** or Buddhism. Many people embrace both religions. A few Japanese are Christians.

FAMOUS FACE

Name: Shigeru Miyamoto
Birthday: November 16, 1952
Hometown: Sonobe, Kyoto, Japan
Famous for: Video game designer for Nintendo who created Mario games, the Legend of Zelda, and other best-selling games

SPEAK JAPANESE

Japanese uses characters instead of letters. However, Japanese words can be written with the English alphabet so you can read them.

ENGLISH	JAPANESE	HOW TO SAY IT
hello	konnichiwa	koh-NEE-chee-wah
goodbye	sayonara	sai-OH-nah-rah
please	onegaishimasu	oh-neh-GAI-she-moss-oo
thank you	arigato	ah-REE-GAW-toh
yes	hai	hi
no	iie	EE-eh

AKIHABARA

SHIBUYA CROSSING
TOKYO

Nearly all Japanese people live in **urban** areas. Tokyo boasts the most populous **metropolitan** area in the world at 38 million people. Japanese cities are very crowded. Houses and apartments tend to be small.

Family is central to the Japanese. Family members feel a strong sense of loyalty to one another. The average Japanese family has one or two children. Single-parent homes have become more common and accepted in recent years. Long work days and **commutes** prevent many parents from spending time with their families. Most spend hours traveling to and from work by train, bus, or subway.

STAYING IN TOUCH

The Japanese have no problem keeping in touch with friends and family. Nearly everyone has a cell phone and Internet connection.

The **traditional** Japanese greeting is a bow. People keep their feet together and their arms by their sides. Lower bows show more respect.

LET'S SHAKE ON IT

Many Japanese people do not expect visitors from Western countries such as the United States to bow to them. They may be fine with a handshake.

GENKAN

Guests in Japanese homes are expected to remove their shoes in an entry area called a *genkan*. It is also polite to bring a gift such as fruit or cake to show respect for the host. Japanese people consider yawning and chewing gum in public to be impolite.

THE SCHOOL OF CRAM

Many Japanese students attend *juku*. These private "cram schools" provide academic support. They help students pass their high school and university entrance exams.

The Japanese place great importance on education. They believe effort and self-discipline determine success, rather than intelligence. Children usually attend school for at least 12 years, though only 9 are required. They focus on math and science. Students must pass a test to enter a public high school. About half of all Japanese youth graduate from college. That usually guarantees a good job.

Service jobs in areas such as finance and education employ most Japanese workers. Others work in manufacturing. Many make cars, which are Japan's biggest **export**. They also produce electronics, tools, and steel.

SHOP WORKER

MANUFACTURING CARS

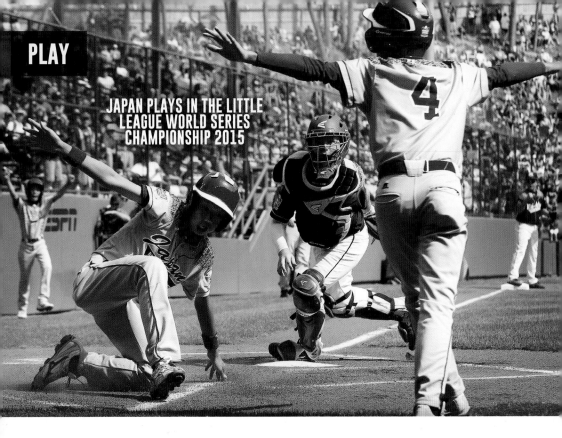

JAPAN PLAYS IN THE LITTLE LEAGUE WORLD SERIES CHAMPIONSHIP 2015

Japan is full of baseball lovers. It is the most popular spectator sport in the country. Other popular sports include soccer, tennis, bowling, and swimming. Japanese people enjoy strolling or jogging through parks to admire spring cherry blossoms or changing leaves in the fall. Skiing and snowboarding are popular in the winter.

THE BEST!

The martial art of judo began in Japan. It was first practiced in Tokyo in 1882. Japan won 38 Olympic gold medals in the sport from 1964 to 2016.

Japanese people also enjoy traditional activities. Many follow the big sumo wrestling tournaments throughout the year. Some practice **martial arts** such as *karate*, *judo*, or *kendo*, a kind of fighting that uses long bamboo sticks.

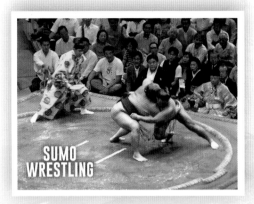

SUMO WRESTLING

OHAJIKI

Ohajiki is a game played on a table or smooth floor with flattened glass pieces or coins spread out.

How to Play:

1. The first player flicks one ohajiki piece toward another with an index finger.

2. The piece that is flicked must hit the targeted piece and separate without touching any other piece.

3. If successful, the player collects the second ohajiki and continues to play. If the shot misses, the next player takes a turn.

4. The player who collects the most ohajiki after all have been hit wins the game!

SLURPING TO PLEASE

It is not unusual to hear Japanese people slurping their food. It is considered a compliment because it shows they are enjoying their meal!

The main meal in Japan is eaten in the evening. Rice and tea are part of nearly every meal. Other common foods in the Japanese diet include pickled vegetables, fruit, and small portions of meat, especially seafood. Also popular are ramen noodles and a soybean soup called *miso*.

The best-known dish of Japan is *sushi*, or rice often served with raw fish or vegetables. A popular food on the island of Kyushu is *basashi*, which is raw horse meat dipped in soy sauce.

SUSHI

BASASHI

OKONOMIYAKI FACE RECIPE

Ingredients:
1 cup flour
2/3 cup water
2 eggs
4 cups cabbage, cut into strips
2 stalks green onions, thinly sliced
6 strips bacon, cut into 3-inch pieces
mayonnaise

Steps:
1. Whisk together flour and water in large bowl.
2. Add eggs, cabbage, and onions, but do not overmix.
3. With an adult, oil a preheated griddle. Divide mixture into two pancakes and add to the griddle.
4. Flatten pancakes with spatula so they are about 0.75 inches (2 centimeters) thick and about 12 inches (30 centimeters) across.
5. Add bacon pieces to create mouth, eyes, and ears for each pancake.
6. After three minutes, flip over both pancakes and cook for four more minutes.
7. Flip pancakes again until firm and brown.
8. Remove to plate and drizzle with mayonnaise.

CELEBRATIONS

Japan celebrates four holidays in one special week every spring. Golden Week runs from April 29 to May 5. It combines Showa Day, Constitution Day, Greenery Day, and Children's Day. Most Japanese people get time off work and school to travel and celebrate.

Another Japanese holiday is *Obon*, or the Lantern Festival. It is held in July or August. Tradition claims that it is when the spirts of the dead return home. Families clean the graves of their **ancestors** and light lanterns to welcome them. Japan also celebrates the cherry blossoms in the spring and rice harvest in the summer. Such events give the people a chance to show love for their country.

OBON

HAPPY NEW YEAR!

New Year's Day is known as *Shogatsu* in Japan. The Japanese celebrate by cleaning their homes and preparing huge dinners. Buddhist temples also ring their bells 108 times to drive out evil.

CHERRY BLOSSOM VIEWING

1635
The Sakoku Edict closes the country so Japanese people cannot leave the country and Europeans cannot enter

1872
A railway connects the cities of Tokyo and Yokohama

ABOUT 500
Buddhism introduced in Japan

1867
Emperor Meiji begins his reign and works to modernize Japan

1941
The United States declares war on Japan after the bombing of Pearl Harbor

1966
The Toyota Corolla is introduced in Japan and later becomes the best-selling car of all time

1890
A new Japanese constitution goes into effect

1905
The end of the Russo-Japanese War results in Japanese control of Korea until 1945

2011
The Great Tohoku Earthquake causes tsunami waves that devastate much of coastal Japan

1945
Atomic bombs destroy Hiroshima and Nagasaki during World War II

Official Name: Japan

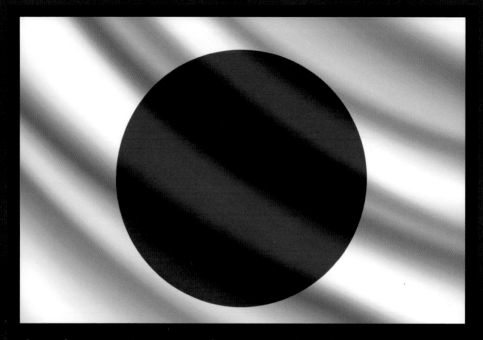

Flag of Japan: The Japanese flag consists of a red circle in the center of a white background. It is known as *Nisshoki*, or "rising sun flag" in the Japanese language. The circle represents the sun goddess *Amaterasu*. Tradition says she founded Japan 2,700 years ago.

Area: 145,914 square miles
(377,915 square kilometers)

Capital City: Tokyo

Important Cities: Yokohama, Kobe, Osaka, Nagoya, Sapporo, Kyoto

Population:
126,702,133 (July 2016)

WHERE
PEOPLE LIVE

COUNTRYSIDE
6.5%

CITY
93.5%

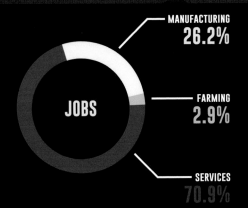

MANUFACTURING
26.2%

JOBS

FARMING
2.9%

SERVICES
70.9%

Main Exports:

iron

steel

plastics

electronics

vehicles

auto parts

National Holiday:
Birthday of Emperor Akihito
(December 23)

Main Language:
Japanese

Form of Government:
parliamentary constitutional monarchy

Title for Country Leaders:
emperor, prime minister

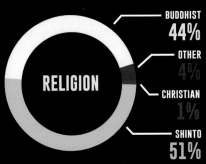

RELIGION

BUDDHIST
44%

OTHER
4%

CHRISTIAN
1%

SHINTO
51%

Many Japanese practice
both Shintoism and Buddhism.

Unit of Money:
Yen

GLOSSARY

ancestors—relatives who lived long ago

commutes—travels to work or school and back

descent—the action of going down

diverse—made up of people or things that are different from one another

dormant—inactive

export—a product sold by one country to another

habitats—lands with certain types of plants, animals, and weather

martial arts—styles and techniques of fighting and self-defense that are practiced as sport

metropolitan—the combined city and suburban area

native—originally from the area or related to a group of people that began in the area

plain—a large area of flat land

service jobs—jobs that perform tasks for people or businesses

Shintoism—a native religion of Japan that honors nature and worships the emperor as a descendant of the sun goddess

traditional—related to customs, ideas, or beliefs handed down from one generation to the next

tsunamis—powerful waves caused by underwater earthquakes

typhoons—powerful storms in the western Pacific Ocean

urban—related to cities and city life

venomous—producing a poisonous substance called venom

volcano—a hole in the earth; when a volcano erupts, hot ash, gas, or melted rock called lava shoots out.

TO LEARN MORE

AT THE LIBRARY

Catel, Patrick. *Japan*. Chicago, Ill.: Heinemann Library, 2012.

Moore, Willamarie. *All About Japan: Stories, Songs, Crafts and Games for Kids.* North Clarendon, Vt.: Tuttle Publishing, 2017.

Murray, Julie. *Japan*. Minneapolis, Minn.: ABDO Publishing Company, 2014.

ON THE WEB

Learning more about Japan is as easy as 1, 2, 3.

1. Go to www.factsurfer.com.

2. Enter "Japan" into the search box.

3. Click the "Surf" button and you will see a list of related web sites.

With factsurfer.com, finding more information is just a click away.

INDEX

The images in this book are reproduced through the courtesy of: Juan Martinez, front cover, pp. 5 (middle bottom), 10 (bottom), 21 (bottom), 29 (coin); Alan Bauman, front cover (flag), pp. 4-5, 5 (bottom), 9, 10 (bottom corner, top), 18, 23 (middle); Raju Soni, p. 5 (top); Philip Maguire, p. 5 (middle top); Brittany McIntosh, pp. 6-7; Krishna Wu, p. 8; Amana Images Inc/ Getty Images, p. 8 (inset); Sakarin Sawadinaka, p. 9 (inset); Redswept, pp. 10-11; Wikipedia, pp. 10 (middle), 26 (top); Vladimir Zhoga, p. 12; Jack Photo, p. 13; Reuters/ Alamy Stock Photo, p. 13 (top); Sean Pavone, pp. 14, 15; StockStudioX, p. 16; imageBROKER/Alamy Stock Photo, p. 17; Batchelder/ Alamy Stock Photo, p. 19 (top); Yoshikazu Tsuno/ Staff/ Getty Images, p. 19 (bottom); Rob Carr/ Staff/ Getty Images, p. 20; Tony Marshall - EMPICS/ Contributor/ Getty Images, p. 20 (bottom); Luciano Lepre/ GLOW Images, p. 21 (top); Johnny Greig, p. 22; Tatiana Bralnina, p. 23 (top); Sakura Photography/ Getty Images, p. 23 (bottom); National Geographic Creative/ Alamy Stock Photo, p. 24; Richie Chan, pp. 24-25; Niday Picture Library/ Alamy Stock Photo, p. 26 (bottom); TTTNIS, p. 27 (top); Ky Cho, p. 29 (currency).